NEGLECTED AREAS
of
PIANO TEACHING

Trevor Barnard

diversions

Diversions Books, Brandon, Vermont, USA MMXVI

Neglected Areas of Piano Teaching

First published in this format in the United Kingdom by Diversions Books,
a division of Divine Art Ltd., in 2008.
Revised edition published 2016
Divine Art Limited, 2 Lady Hamilton Drive, Swarland, Morpeth, NE65 9HH, UK
Published in the USA by:
Diversions LLC, 333 Jones, Drive, Brandon, VT 05733, USA

www.divineartrecords.com

Edited, formatted and typeset by Divine Art

Library of Congress Control Number: 2009943502

British Library Cataloguing in Publication Data available

ISBN: 978-0-991-2232-3-7

CONTENTS

Short musical examples, to which the text refers, are printed at the end of each chapter.

TREVOR BARNARD - A biography

British born Australian pianist, Trevor Barnard, began piano lessons at the age of four and while still very young studied at the Royal Academy of Music, London. This was followed by several years of private tuition with Herbert Fryer, a student of Ferruccio Busoni. At the age of sixteen he was awarded the ARCM Diploma in Piano, and later won a full scholarship to the Royal College of Music, London. Subsequently, he undertook intensive masterclass study with Harold Craxton.

Between 1967 and 1972 Trevor Barnard lived in the USA, where he was a faculty member of the New England Conservatory in Boston (1968-1972); and Pianist-in-Residence to Boston University Radio (1967-1971), when he recorded the complete cycles of Beethoven and Mozart Piano Sonatas, plus other major works in the piano repertoire. In addition to many concert appearances he gave several half-hour recitals for TV in Boston and New York City. In moving to Melbourne in 1972 he became piano tutor at Monash University. From 1974 to 1988 he taught full-time consecutively at the Melbourne State College and the Melbourne College of Advanced Education, and from 1989 at The University of Melbourne until his retirement at the end of 2003.

As a concert artist Trevor Barnard has appeared with the London Symphony, the Philharmonia, the City of Birmingham Symphony, the Bournemouth Symphony, and various BBC orchestras. In Australia he has toured and broadcast frequently for the ABC. On three occasions he was the featured concerto soloist on their TV programme WORLD OF MUSIC (works being the Bliss/Schumann Concerti and the Mozart *Concert Rondo, K. 382*, films of which are in the ABC's permanent archives). A noted chamber music player, he appeared on every occasion from 1975 to 1994 in the former annual Melbourne chamber music festival MUSIC IN THE ROUND.

His discography includes the Arthur Bliss *Piano Concerto* with the Philharmonia and Sir Malcolm Sargent for EMI (re-issued in England by the Divine Art Record Company), and a solo album for the World Record Club *An Introduction to Piano Music* (also re-issued, in an expanded version, by Divine Art under the title *A Piano Odyssey*). American composer - Richard St. Clair, and Australian composers - Geoffrey Allen, Michael Bertram and Felix Werder, have written works especially for him. The first of the Felix Werder works appears in Trevor's début solo CD on the Divine Art label of J.S. Bach transcriptions and modern Australian piano music.

His second CD for the same company features the Arthur Bliss *Sonata* and the première commercial recording of the *24 Preludes, Op. 37* by Busoni. Trevor's next solo release by Divine Art of Australian compositions includes the Dorian Le Gallienne *Sonata* and with it, appearing on commercial disc for the first time, the other Felix Werder work and remaining Australian works that are dedicated to him.

continued...

A further recording of him performing the virtuoso William Lovelock *Sonata for Saxophone and Piano* with Australia's greatest classical saxophonist, Peter Clinch, was released by Divine Art in July 2006.

In addition to *Neglected Areas of Piano Teaching* Trevor Barnard is the author of an American-published repertoire guide *A Practical Guide to Solo Piano Music*. He has also contributed several pedagogical articles to the leading U.S. keyboard journal *Clavier* and its successor, *Clavier Companion*.

Amongst other activities, Trevor has served as a regular contributor and reviewer for the (Australian) *Music Teacher International* magazine, an examiner for the Australian Music Examinations Board, and an adviser on the piano performance requirements for the Victorian Certificate of Education. He is also an experienced adjudicator, and, along with many eisteddfodau, has adjudicated the ABC Young Performers' competition on a number of occasions.

PREFACE TO SECOND EDITION

During a career teaching piano at all levels and in three countries for over forty years, a number of pedagogical areas that I perceived as being rather neglected in mainstream teaching became an important part of my work.

As a result, in the late 1990s and early into the new millennium, I submitted my findings in a series of articles that were published in the U.S. journal *Clavier*, its successor *Clavier Companion* and the (Australian) *Music Teacher International* magazine. These articles have now been collated into the present volume. I thank those publications for their support in this.

Trevor Barnard
Melbourne, Australia, 2016

Recordings by Trevor Barnard published by Divine Art

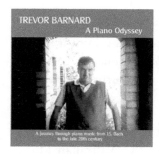

Diversions DDV24125
"A Piano Odyssey"
A journey through piano music from the early 18th to the late 20th century, with music by J.S.Bach, Schubert, Beethoven, Mendelssohn, Schumann, Chopin, Grieg, Rachmaninoff, Debussy, Albéniz, Bartók, Gershwin, Sutherland, Sculthorpe, Butterley, Bertram, Dargaville and Werder

Diversions 24106
Sir Arthur Bliss: Piano Concerto
The pioneering 1962 recording which shot Trevor Barnard to fame.
With Sir Malcolm Sargent conducting the Philharmonia Orchestra
"Barnard..plays with….scintillating brilliance.. the central movement is beautifully handled... some of the most precious minutes I have spent in recent months" – Fanfare

Divine Art 25005
"Bach Transcriptions and Modern Australian Piano Music"

Featuring Bach, arranged by Busoni and Hess, and modern music by Werder, Butterley and Sutherland

"Eloquent and skilful advocacy" - Gramophone

Divine Art 25011
Bliss: Piano Sonata
Busoni: 24 Preludes, Op. 37

"Barnard's playing is full-bodied, with generous pedal, a weighty tone and a fine ability to control atmosphere and emotional temperature." – BBC Music Magazine (★★★★)

Divine Art 25017
"Blue Wrens"
Modern Australian Piano Music by Geoffrey Allen, Felix Werder, Dorian Le Gallienne, Tim Dargaville and Michael Bertram.

"Superbly interpreted by Trevor Barnard, who plays with feeling, sensitivity and enormous conviction… a splendid recording" – The Studio

Divine Art, Diversions, Metier and Athene CDs are produced by Divine Art and available at record dealers worldwide, or direct through our webstore:

www.divineartrecords.com

Basic Pedaling Techniques

Good pedaling is one of the most confusing aspects of learning to play the piano. Whilst instruction manuals abound in suggestions on teaching the instrument, there is not as much available on the subject of pedaling as piano teachers would reasonably expect, so developments in this area are often acquired by instinct rather than through training. There is no reason why any young student who is able to reach the pedals from a normal sitting position should delay in developing good pedal habits. There are four basic pedaling techniques, two of which are usually used by intermediate students and two that are essential in more advanced repertoire.

The pedal on the right is called the damper pedal because it moves the entire row of dampers away from the strings so notes continue to sound even though the keys are not depressed. It is misleading to call the damper pedal the loud or sustaining pedal, and some teachers incorrectly refer to it as the sostenuto pedal, which is actually the middle pedal on a grand piano. The damper pedal is used in legato playing to connect notes as well as for color.

Direct pedaling is the first pedaling technique students should learn. For this the pedal and keys are depressed simultaneously and released together; the foot makes a single down-up motion to separate the notes and next foot depression. This technique adds color to the sound, but it can also be used in legato areas where extra color is of less relevance. Direct pedaling in its most basic form is found in the Sonata in C Major, Op. 2, no. 3 by Beethoven. In this piece (see *example 1*), the pedal should be depressed while playing each chord and then released to keep the chords separate. Instead of an unsatisfactory dry quality, the sound acquires a richness of color.

For more extended passages, depress the pedal and notes at the start of each indicated half-bar and release the pedal one beat later (*example 2*).

In *Sechs kleine Klavierstücke*, Op. 19, by Schoenberg (*example 3*), it is possible to play all the notes of the last eighth beat in measure 2 with the left hand, but it is a simple matter to play the F♯ with the right hand and use the pedal to make the notes legato. The relatively high pitches avoid the excessive resonance that might intrude on the sound.

Intermediate students can develop this relatively easy technique by practicing a series of detached, random chords slowly, and depressing and releasing the pedal. They can increase the speed as coordination becomes more comfortable, then play this short exercise from Bartók's *Mikrokosmos*, Volume 2 (*example 4*).

The sound will be fuller if students pedal the half-note chords and final whole-note chord.

Next they might play *Moon Walk*, a piece in an entirely different style by Australian composer Larry Sitsky (*example 5*). The composer gives specific pedal instructions to capture the character of the music

Of course, musical texts frequently show little guidance for pedaling, and the player has to take artistic initiative. Knowledge and experience will prove most useful in discerning how to pedal in less obvious situations, as in the Waltz from *Lyric Pieces*, Op. 12, where Grieg gives only general indications for the pedal. To omit it completely would result in too much dryness overall, yet the damper pedal should still be used sparingly. The dance rhythm would be enhanced by the fuller sound, but any excess pedal will take vitality away from the gentle flow of the music.

Even though the direct pedaling technique would work, the pedaling I suggest in **example 6** will never be completely definitive under such circumstances; such is the joy of interpretation.

The second technique is legato pedaling, also called indirect pedaling. The main purpose is to move from one note or chord to another note or chord without a gap in the sound when the fingers cannot connect the notes of chords easily. For a pedal change that is free from any blurriness, pedal again immediately after playing a new note or chord. An earlier change may cause a break in the sound, or the previous chord may linger. If the change is delayed at all, the sound will be blurry. The entire action leaves little room for a timing error.

A good exercise for students is to play a chord and depress the damper pedal simultaneously, then play another chord but wait two seconds before changing the pedal. With a series of chords there will be extreme blurriness from the long wait between pedal changes, and students will get used to the movements.

For the actual pedal change it is important to execute the up-down movement without excess noise from the foot that would detract from the music. It is best not to lift the foot from the pedal at any time to retain maximum control.

A fine example for practicing *legato* pedaling is Chopin's Prelude in C minor from the set of 24 Preludes (**example 7**). The slow pace gives students plenty of space to pedal between chords. The pedal changes in the bass at the fortissimo level will indicate in no uncertain terms whether the foot and fingers are synchronized.

After learning these first two pedaling techniques, students should study a piece that combines both. Schumann's *Kinderszenen* has challenging pedal markings that will be easy for students who have practiced the preparatory exercises and gradually increased the tempo. See *example 8*.

One important variation in the legato pedaling technique arises when a chord that should be played legato cannot have all the notes covered by the fingers. If the performer changes the pedal after playing the first note, the chord will sound legato but the bass note will not be held. In Chopin's Nocturne in C minor, Op. 48, no. 1, (**example 9**) the chord spreads start from the bottom bass note and proceeds to the top right hand notes.

The answer is to use direct pedaling. Completely releasing the pedal and subsequently depressing it again with the start of the new chord will retain the lowest notes. With practice the gap in the sound will be so miniscule that listeners will be unaware of it.

The third technique, half-pedaling, is identical to legato pedaling except that the pedal only lifts partially instead of completely. The word "half" is approximate, and the pedal lift will vary with each instrument. In his book *Etudes for Piano Teachers* (Oxford University Press), Stewart Gordon states that with half-pedaling "the dampers are but partially in contact with the strings, providing some but not complete dampening", and in *Pumping Ivory* (Ekay Music), Robert Dumm explains that a half pedal "permits the dampers to lightly graze the vibrating strings, trimming but not stopping the sound." Performers usually develop a feel for half-pedaling after a fairly short period. A climactic moment in *La cathédrale engloutie* from Debussy's Préludes, Book 1 (**example 10**), illustrates half-pedaling.

Note that the bottom low C bass note has to last through the succeeding chords. Obviously, full legato pedal changes for each harmonic change will not hold the original bass note; half changes are a satisfactory solution that enhance the music and meet the composer's intentions. Another choice is to use the sostenuto pedal here.

If there are a number of harmonic shifts above a held pedal note, then the half-pedaling technique is the correct option. However, if there is some filigree over a harmonic background that causes muddiness, then flutter pedaling, the fourth technique, works better. Debussy's *Feuilles mortes* from the Préludes, Book 2, has a series of quick, short movements with the foot in combination with relatively fast-moving notes, which causes the dampers to regularly brush the strings. Rapid raising and depressing of the damper pedal gives the music continuity and avoids unpleasant blurriness –see *example 11*.

Another quite dissimilar example is Grieg's famous *Notturno*, a popular piece among young students, who enjoy its expressive charm. However, this particular section (see *example 12*) is often a cause for frustration.

Unless flutter pedaling is used, the sound will be either empty or blurred. Young students can learn flutter pedaling with this piece. This takes a high degree of control, and teachers should be encouraging.

Pedaling should not be a neglected area of piano teaching, but I am not aware of any music school that includes pedaling tests as part of its requirements; such an initiative would be a major breakthrough in recognizing this important pedagogical area.

Trevor Barnard helps student Silvana Angilletta with half-pedaling.

"Good pedaling is one of the most confusing aspects of learning to play the piano."

Basic Pedaling Techniques – examples

Example 1: Beethoven - Sonata in C major, Op. 2, no. 3

Example 2: Beethoven - Sonata in C major, Op. 2, no 3

Example 3: Schoenberg - from *Sechs kleine Klavierstücke*, Op. 19

Example 4: Bartók - from *Mikrokosmos*, Volume 2

Example 5: Sitsky - *Moon Walk*

Example 6: Grieg - Waltz (*Lyric Pieces*, Op. 12, no. 2)

Example 7: Chopin - Prelude in C minor, Op. 28, no. 20

Example 8: Schumann - from *Kinderszenen*, Op. 15

Example 9: Chopin – Nocturne in C minor, Op. 48, no. 1

Example 10: Debussy – Préludes, book 1: *La cathédrale engloutie*

Example 11: Debussy – Préludes, book 2: *Feuilles mortes*

Measures 3-4

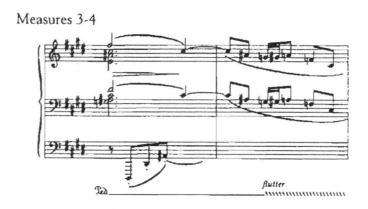

Example 12: Grieg – *Notturno* from Lyric Pieces, Op. 54

Equal Training for Both Hands

The first years of instruction often favor development of the right hand, as students practice scales and arpeggios conscientiously. Much beginning repertoire has the melody in the right hand, leaving the left hand a second-class citizen, neglected and underdeveloped, even in students who are left-handed. This often leads to later coordination problems when the melody is passed to the left hand as the right plays a discreet accompaniment.

The hands should be equal partners from the outset, with scales practiced in parallel, in contrary motion, and cross-handed, to develop the left hand equally well. One exercise might exchange the melody and accompaniment between the hands every few bars. Another exercise is to play a slow scale in octaves, alternating the dominant sound every few notes, as shown in *example 13*.

Fugues are excellent for advanced students because the counterpoint is played by both hands. The goal is to develop an ambidextrous pianist both technically and musically, using different weights of touch simultaneously and carrying this at will. It is not just a matter of developing equal strength in both hands but training the brain to make decisions that suit the music.

In Bach's Minuet in G major from the *Anna Magdalena Notebook* the eighth notes alternate from right hand to left hand, as shown by arrows (see *example 14*).

The melody is in the treble clef throughout, but the left hand eighth notes provide rhythmic continuity. Practice shifting the emphasis between the hands, keeping the eighth notes smooth during the change and coordinating those notes in one hand with the quarter notes in the other .

Left and right hands share the melody in Kabalevsky's *Clowning*, Op. 27, no. 10 (*example 15*). Each three-note figure contains a left-hand melody note followed by a right-hand melody note and a right-hand accompaniment note.

A different weight on each note will enhance the texture but this takes balance and coordination. Practice the piece several ways, first emphasizing the left-hand note, then the first right-hand note, or the second right-hand note. Although the left hand plays on the downbeat, the right hand plays a subdivision of the beat that determines each subsequent left-hand note. Before trying to slur the two right-hand notes as written, practice the passage as if the slur extended to the next left-hand note, as shown by the dotted slur in the example above. Once the hands are well coordinated, return to the original articulation.

The pieces in Béla Bartók's *Mikrokosmos* were conceived with pedagogy in mind and develop the right and left hands equally. No. 22, "Imitation and Counterpoint", from Volume 1 is a simple example of ambidextrous, independent hands that still play together, as shown by the extract in *example 16*.

Bartók marked an overall dynamic of *forte*, but the bare single notes should not sound abrasive. With that in mind, play the louder part between *mf* and *mp*, and the softer part at a *p* level. The inserted arrows show how the musical emphasis shifts from measure to measure. In no. 24, "Pastorale", also from Volume 1, Bartók uses strettos; the second part overtakes the first in the midst of its statement. To create a smooth dialogue, shift the emphasis early, as indicated in *example 17*.

In contrast to Bartók's contrapuntal approach, the homophonic style of the Classical period often relegates one hand to a very minor role indeed. This is where ambidexterity comes to the rescue and reinvigorates the music. In

Haydn's Sonata no. 53 in E minor (*example 18*), movement three, the Alberti bass occupies the left hand throughout most of the movement:

If the right hand plays with too much emphasis, the left hand will sound mechanical and inhibited, eroding the effect of a clear and well-shaped right hand. In contrast, briefly transferring attention to the left hand results in greater rhythmic definition and a sense of dialogue between the hands, revitalizing the performance. Here again, the arrows indicate shifts of emphasis. Unlike the Bartók, where the shifts are largely established by the music, these are more subjective. A performer can alter their position in the score but still follow the principle. In this example and those that follow, even small shifts will vary the balance between the hands.

Stephen Briggs keeps hands in balance as Trevor Barnard coaches

While the dreamy, Romantic nature of Chopin's Nocturne in E minor, Op. 72, no. 1 differs from previous examples, the same

principles apply, as shown in *example 19*.

A weak left hand may not detract from the rhythm, but it will certainly result in a marked loss of sonority and musical intensity. As in the Haydn, the arrows show one idea of how to shift the emphasis. In different performances of the passage, the shifts occur in different spots.

Example 20, an extract from Gershwin's Prelude No. 2 focuses on a melody in the left hand, accompanied by double notes in the right hand. When Gershwin suggests reversing the hands as an optional version, he seems to anticipate the balance problem inherent in the piece.

With all due respect, this is the easy way out for a student pianist. Gershwin's indication of *mf* for the left-hand melody and *p* for the right-hand accompaniment clearly establishes the balance between the hands, but the margin between these dynamics is still too narrow. To avoid bumpiness and prevent the right hand from obscuring the melody in any way, play the right-hand notes as softly as possible. This improves left-hand clarity which should not be a problem if the pianist is already ambidextrous. If not, this is a marvelous goal for the less-skilled player, Even in this extreme example of one hand dominating the other, some slight interaction should still take place to prevent the right hand from disappearing altogether. Although it continues to play a supporting role, the right hand should make itself known from time to time. The arrows show one suggestion for shifting emphasis from hand to hand.

A similar phrase in Chopin's Prelude in B minor, Op. 28, no. 6, will challenge students to phrase, follow dynamics, and use articulation in the left-hand melody. See *example 21*.

Although the left hand plays the melody almost throughout, the right hand takes over from the end of measure 6 through measure 8. The right hand also comes to the fore when the left hand arrives on a long note in measures 14, 22 and 25, with a shift from left-hand to right-hand dominance. For the balance of the piece the right hand is subordinate to the left-hand melody.

Attention to the balance between the hands will reduce coordination problems, as in Beethoven's Sonata in C minor, Op. 13 *Pathétique*, where the left hand has fast-moving figures in tandem with a lively right hand. The performer should use the left hand as an anchor to keep the hands together.

Using **example 22**, focus on the first bass note of each measure, pausing slightly before placing the downbeat. Lean on the left-hand fifth finger, bringing the weight of the forearm behind the note and, using it as a pivot, spring or bounce off gently through the remaining left-hand notes of the measure. The right-hand notes should be played much more softly than the left-hand notes so that there is a definite feeling of guidance from the left hand.

In Rachmaninoff's Prelude in C♯ minor, Op. 3, no. 2, which is shown in **example 23**, the right hand should be the guide through the rapid exchange of chords, to avoid having this become a boxing match between the hands.

Coordinate the hands by leaning on the accented right-hand chord at the start of each half measure, bouncing off onto the other five chords in each group with a lighter touch. Disregard the accents on beats two and four until the chords are comfortable. This change of emphasis allows the passage to flow.

Even some professional pianists play the piano with the right hand dominant, but it is never too late to address the problem, especially with students in the early stages. If they become ambidextrous early in their training they will play with greater control in advanced pieces, making interpretive decisions based upon the music rather than their physical limitations.

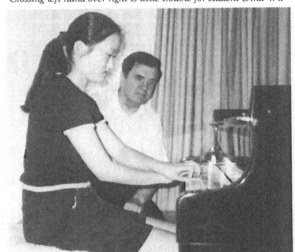

Crossing left hand over right is little trouble for student Dina Wu

"The hands should be equal partners from the outset"

Equal Training for Both Hands – examples

Example 13: C major scale in octaves

Example 14: Bach - Minuet in G major (Anna Magdalena Notebook)

Example 15: Kabalevsky - *Clowning*, Op. 27, no. 10

Example 16: Bartók - *Mikrokosmos*, Volume 1, no. 22 "Imitation and Counterpoint"

Example 17: Bartok - *Mikrokosmos*, Volume 1, no. 24 "Pastorale"

Example 18: Haydn - Sonata no. 53 in E minor (third movement)

Example 19: Chopin - Nocturne in E minor, Op. 72, no. 1

Example 20: Gershwin – Prelude No. 2

Example 21: Chopin – Prelude in B minor, Op. 28, no. 6

Example 22: Beethoven – Sonata in C minor, Op. 13 *Pathétique*

Example 23: Rachmaninoff – Prelude in C sharp minor, Op. 3, no. 2

Early Lessons in Phrasing

There is no reason why beginning students cannot learn how to add expressive phrasing to music, regardless of the tempo or style of a piece, and especially in fast passages. For an easy way to teach phrasing, have students think of phrases as musical sentences. I have beginners read prose or poetry aloud, watching for punctuation marks, commas and periods, which are similar to phrase indications in music. In the first reading of a poem students speak without expression, but the second time through they add inflections.

After two readings of a poem I discuss the subtle improvements in nuances with students and relate these concepts to music. On the third reading of the poem, to avoid sounding mechanical, students vary the tempo. I compare this uneven pace of the voice to the steady ticking of a metronome and note how deviations from the metronome are similar to rubato in music.

I introduce musical phrasing using Béla Bartók's *Mikrokosmos*, Volume 1, (*example 24*) having students shape the piece with added crescendos and diminuendos, just as they added expression to the poem. In the second phrase the peak of the crescendo deliberately falls on a descending note to convey the idea that not all crescendos rise in pitch.

Conversely I included, for additional practice, a rise in pitch for one of the diminuendos as well as twice as many crescendos and diminuendos within the same framework of two four-measure phrases, as shown in *example 25*.

An expressive piece, such as "Melodie" from Robert Schumann's *Album for the Young*, is ideal for developing phrasing skills in early-intermediate students. Schumann divides the opening two four-measure phrases into four two-measure phrases. To help shape the melodic line, I added crescendo and diminuendo markings to measure three followed by another diminuendo (*example 26*).

For this passage the pattern of crescendos and diminuendos can be altered to create yet another interpretation (*example 27*). Both examples will help students play a crescendo that falls in pitch and a diminuendo that rises in pitch.

The left-hand accompaniment should help the right hand highlight the tune by briefly playing out the accompaniment. In the second line of "Melodie", accents on the first beats of measures 5, 6 and 7 call for a diminuendo over notes that fall in pitch. To avoid a bumpy effect a slight fermata, combined with a gentle stress on the accented notes, helps to smoothly articulate the phrase without over-accentuation. Switching the musical focus to the left hand during the right hand rests on beat four will encourage students to interpret the phrase musically, as shown in *example 28*.

Pieces by the American composer Robert Muczynski are well suited to intermediate-level students interested in atonal music. His work *Diversions*, Op. 23, lacks a tonal center and has no overall phrase marks. Students have to take some initiative in phrasing the piece. A considerable amount of musical detail is already present – slurs, tenutos, accents, crescendos, diminuendos and staccatos – to give a good start for a musical interpretation, as you can see in *example 29*.

To highlight phrase structure I show students how to use a small pause at the point where one phrase ends and another begins; the music will sound overly phrased if the pause is too long. A number of slurs and phrases in this piece start on up-beats, which take attention away from a mechanical performance. Even if this were not the case, it is generally true that some stress and sufficient length should be added on up-beats. Some contemporary composers omit dynamics, phrase marks, time signatures or bar lines, leaving these to the player to add.

Unmusical phrasing of fast passages may stem from the unmusical way students practice scales and technical studies. Students who learn to add interpretive ideas to pieces as they develop technique in the beginning years are more likely to be musically imaginative later.

The worst examples of inconsistent phrasing are found in scale-like passages or on such ornaments as turns, mordents and trills. A very fast scale, turn, mordent or trill should first be played slowly and melodically, then gradually brought up to speed without ever sounding mechanical. Suggest varying where the crescendos and diminuendos occur and emphasizing different notes of a scale, which can be combined with rhythmic variations.

The first movement of the Sonata in G major, Op. 49, no. 2 by Beethoven (*example 30*) has scale runs that are often played metronomically with consistent accents, rendering the music expressionless.

To escape from an overly rhythmic sound, students can learn how to shape the music by emphasizing different notes, as shown in *example 31*. Some stress on off-beat notes helps the music sound expressive, not metronomic. Using tenuto marks instead of accents keeps performers from adding too much stress to notes.

In measure 44, the first note of the left-hand scale is on the up-beat (see *example 32*). Emphasize this note and the two other off-beat notes in this legato run, which is played twice, an octave apart. Following are alternative ways to add interest to the passage.

Students who struggle with ornaments on scalar passages should purchase *The World's Greatest Sonatinas*, edited by Maurice Hinson, which spells out the articulations of measured trills and mordents. In the *Andante* movement from the Sonatina in G major, Hob. XVI:11 by Franz Joseph Haydn, students usually accent the first note of each trill, which overly emphasizes the rhythm. We see this in *example 33*.

To make the melody more interesting, shift the emphasis to the off-beat notes, as in *example 34*.

This approach also works with a longer measured trill, as in Clementi's *Allegro* movement from the Sonatina in G major, Op. 36, no. 2 (*example 35*).

For melodic sounding upper and lower mordents emphasize the third note of three-note mordents and the second note of two-note mordents. The baroque-style upper mordent in bar 42 of Benda's Sonatina in A minor (*example 36*) should be played melodically, despite a fairly quick execution, by adding some emphasis to the second E rather than the first.

A slight emphasis on the second note of the lower mordent in Haydn's G major Sonatina should also be adopted for a musical result, as I show in *example 37*.

In Beethoven's Rondo movement from the F major Sonatina the conventional turn can be interpreted in three alternative ways. The obvious emphasis on the first note produces an overly rhythmic or mechanical interpretation. Some emphasis on the second note, as shown in **example 38** reduces the rhythmic accent and encourages more expression as does a small crescendo towards the third note and a decrescendo to the next main beat.

This same principle can be applied to make longer phrases by connecting shorter ones. In Bach's Minuet in G, emphasizing the third beat in several measures connects phrases and highlights the overall contour, and adds variety by avoiding constant downbeat emphasis. I show this in **example 39**.

Balanced piano study includes pieces that help students to develop both musically and technically. Learning to phrase is often neglected in the early years of study when it is especially valuable to develop musicianship skills. Beyond playing all the right notes and rhythms, encourage students to interpret their pieces musically so that years later the idea of interpretation is not a mystery.

"Learning to phrase is often neglected in the early years"

Early Lessons in Phrasing – examples

Example 24: Bartók - from *Mikrokosmos*, Volume 1

Example 25: Bartók - from *Mikrokosmos*, Volume 1

Example 26: Schumann - "Melodie" from *Album for the Young*, Op. 68

Example 27: Schumann - "Melodie" from *Album for the Young*, Op. 68

Example 28: Schumann – "Melodie" from *Album for the Young*, Op. 68

Example 29: Muczynski - *Diversions*, Op. 23

Example 30: Beethoven - Sonata in G major, Op. 49, no. 2

Example 31: Beethoven - Sonata in G major, Op. 49, no. 2

Example 32: Beethoven - Sonata in G major, Op. 49, no. 2

Example 33: Haydn – Sonatina in G major, Hob. XVI:11 (*Andante*)

Example 34: Haydn – Sonatina in G major, Hob. XVI:11

18

Example 35: Clementi - Sonatina in G major, Op. 36, no. 2

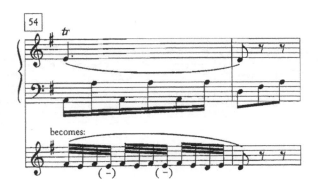

Example 36: Benda - Sonatina in A minor

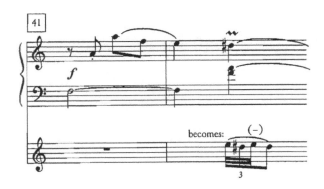

Example 37: Haydn - Sonatina in G major, Hob. XVI:11

Example 38: Beethoven (Attrib.) - Sonatina in F major, Anh.5

Example 39: Bach - Minuet in G (*Anna Magdalena Notebook*)

How Soft is Soft?

After more than 30 years of teaching and working with colleagues, I believe some teachers pay too little attention to interpreting very soft and very loud dynamics, from *pppp*, *ffff*, and *sfff*. Problems with dynamics may result from practicing long hours alone without coaching or by not recognizing when a composer writes excessive dynamic markings. In Chopin's Nocturne in G minor, Op. 37, no. 1 (*example 40*), the change from *pp* to *ff* is too extreme in the musical context. This is a common dilemma for musicians who try to be true to the printed score, yet the music line sounds off.

The *pp* marking at the start of the passage is reasonable for the dreamy character of the music. In measure 71, however, the composer writes an excessive dynamic, *ff*, an increase of five dynamic levels from the preceding measure. By raising the volume only two or three levels to *mp* or *mf*, the music retains an intimate quality and avoids sounding harsh.

A less extreme example is the passage (*example 41*) from Edvard Grieg's "Wedding Day at Troldhaugen" in *Lyric Pieces*, Op. 65, no. 6, which leaps suddenly from *pp* to *f*. The composer obviously wants increased brightness, but for the thin texture of the music a marking somewhere between *mp* and *mf* is more appropriate. It is worth remembering that *p* and *pp* markings are often not all that soft.

To learn to convey dynamics, students might find it helpful to imagine an actor on stage reciting the lines of a play to an audience, speaking in a larger-than-life voice instead of a conversational tone so that the audience easily picks up his intentions. In the same way a pianist projects dynamics to convey the emotion of the music. To help students I recommend that the dynamic levels from *ppp* to *mp* be raised up a maximum of one level higher, depending on the context of the music and physical surroundings, so the notes sufficiently sound.

Training students to use dynamics should take place from the start of musical instruction with scales practiced slowly at all levels from *ppp* to *fff*. When practicing with the hands together, each hand could play at a different dynamic level, then exchange levels until the hands become independent. This could be applied to such beginning pieces as the "Imitation and Inversion", no. 23 from Bartók's *Mikrokosmos*, Volume 1, seen in *example 42*.

The piece is marked *f* throughout, although this is a little strong for single-note lines in each hand. It might be prudent to consider a *mf* level to avoid a harsh sound. Unless a student is ambidextrous it is difficult to play louder with the left hand than the right hand, but there are steps to overcome this. First play the entire piece *f* in both hands, then with the right hand *f* and the left hand *p*, then switch the dynamic levels in each hand. A final exercise is to alternate the dynamic balance between the hands every three bars.

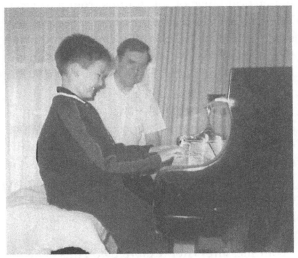

Trevor Barnard with student Yoo Jin Germaine

In Robert Schumann's *Kinderszenen*, Op. 15, no. 12, (**example 43**) the change from *p* in measure 1 to *pp* in measure 9 becomes troublesome because of the thicker chords. Although using the soft pedal in measure 9 alleviates some of the difficulty, a firm-sounding *p* (about halfway between *p* and *mp*) in both hands will project both the single notes and chords at the opening and give greater dynamic contrast nine measures later.

The left hand should play with a gentle firmness so the top notes in the right-hand melody stand out in a cantabile manner. Practically speaking the overall dynamic level here is between *pp* and *p*. The use of the soft pedal changes the timbral quality on a grand piano as well as muffling the sound to some extent, which should help to control and articulate the chords.

The dynamic mark of *ppp* is on the borderline of being an indistinct dynamic level compared to well-defined *pp* and *p* levels. Music marked with *pppp* or more usually results in inaudible sounds, which only the performer hears.

Sergei Rachmaninoff tends to use extreme dynamics, such as those in *Mélodie*, Op. 3, no. 3, an intermediate-level piece that has a wide and impractical range of soft sounds from *p* to *pppp*. The *mf* opening, as we see in **example 44**, suggests a bold melodic line in the left hand that is consistent with the Romantic warmth of this composer's works.

The piece ebbs and flows until the final section. Although the composer specifies a more contrasting and hushed version of the main material, the *pp* to *pppp* marking is definitely not feasible. One inconsistency is the *pp* on the first quarter note followed by a sudden change to *pppp* on the second beat, shown in **example 45**.

Four measures later (**example 46**), this extreme change is exacerbated by a small crescendo culminating in *ppp*.

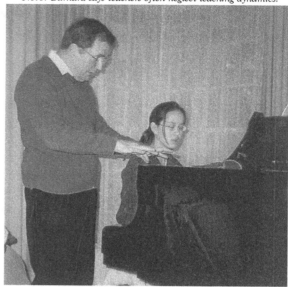

Trevor Barnard says teachers often neglect teaching dynamics.

At the other end of the dynamic range, this composer uses *ffff* to get extreme intensity from performers, but it is not always helpful. Thick chords at such an extreme dynamic should be played carefully and without forcing the sound to an abrasive level. Similar to raising all soft dynamics from *pp* to *mp* up a notch, dynamics from *mf* up to *fff* should also increase, using discretion. To avoid harshness I suggest lightening the lower voices, allowing the top note to stand out in a cantabile manner.

In highly intense moments discretion should be followed, as in Edvard Grieg's "Wedding-day at Troldhaugen" (**example 47**). Here *fff* distorts the sound and is unnecessary; *ff* serves the music adequately. Grieg raises the dynamic level to no louder than *f* prior to this passage; at the *a tempo* he chooses *fff* instead of *ff*, making the most of this highly intense moment. It is almost an over-reaction. The weight of the surges in the left hand will complement the right hand only by lightening the lower voices of the right hand. The right hand is written with thin textures and relatively high on the keyboard so there is no justification to force the sound in any way. The overall dynamic support takes place in the left hand and any attempt by the right hand to match the volume adds an unpleasant, abrasive quality to the sound.

Rachmaninoff's Prelude in C♯ minor, Op. 3, no. 2, as we can see in *example 48*, stakes a strong claim for having the most extravagant dynamic levels in the entire piano repertoire.

Even though this is an emotional piece, the range of *ppp* to *sffff* far exceeds the necessary dynamics to convey the expressive power of the music. Early on in measure 3, the first exaggerated dynamic of *ppp* appears. A *pp* is all the contrast necessary to set off the opening *ff*. Measures 9 and 13 use a similar dynamic that is out of context. Reducing the dynamic one level is helpful here. The *ppp* pertains to chordal figures, which should be played firmly *pp* so all notes sound with sufficient conviction and carrying power.

The climax of the Prelude, shown in *example 49*, begins *fff*, played intensely with broadened phrases and rubato to give a sense of spontaneity to the music. The passage begins fairly high in the treble region of the keyboard, further supporting the argument to not force the sound.

Restrained loudness by reducing the dynamic to between *f* and *ff*, combined with logical pacing, will communicate the musical message. All this is infinitely preferable to a continuing decibel level of harsh sounds.

The final two measures of the section, each marked with an *sfff*, again call for common sense and some expertise with playing *sforzando*. Any *sf* can be performed either by giving the note or chord extra emphasis, or by slightly delaying the note or chord, which automatically implies an accent, or by using a combination of both approaches, which I recommend here. Some restraint of *sfff* guarantees the richness of the sound of the bare octaves. Therefore, these chords should be played no louder than *ff* with the right hand at a softer level than the left hand to avoid any hint of harshness. The richer succeeding chords, marked *ff*, should be a little lighter in contrast, though played with a more uniform dynamic in both hands, somewhere between *f* and *ff*.

This is not the end of the story, as far as Rachmaninoff's use of excessive dynamics in this piece is concerned. At the return of the **A** section (the piece is in ternary form), the composer leaves the pianist with little doubt as to the dynamics, as we can see in *example 50*. He uses the rather odd sequence of *fff pesante* and *sfff* in successive measures, showing little logic here. The *sfff* continues for over a page, further exacerbated by repeated accents above each eighth-note beat. The last page of the piece, marked *dim.*, offers relief from the *sfff*. In the final measure, marked *ppp*, there is a sense of moderation. The pianist should carefully observe the marking and yet be sure that all the notes of the last chord are heard.

Dynamics should always be performed within the context of the music. All *ff* and *fff* passages should be played with discretion. I know of no music school that includes specific guidelines on the interpretation of dynamic markings. Such an initiative would be helpful to all pianists from intermediate to advanced, many of whom are ill-informed in this area.

"Some composers indicate excessive dynamics"

How Soft is Soft? – examples

Example 40: Chopin - Nocturne in G minor, Op. 37, no. 1

Example 41: Grieg - "Wedding-day at Troldhaugen" (*Lyric Pieces,* Op. 65, no. 6)

Example 42: Bartók - "Imitation and Inversion" (*Mikrokosmos*, Volume 1)

Example 43: Schumann - *Kinderszenen*, Op. 15, no. 12

Example 44: Rachmaninoff - *Mélodie*, Op. 3, no. 3

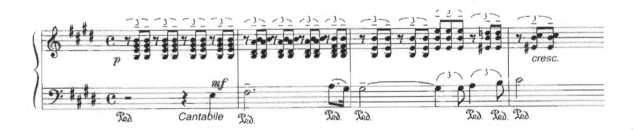

Example 45: Rachmaninoff - *Mélodie*, Op. 3, no. 3

Example 46: Rachmaninoff - *Mélodie*, Op. 3, no. 3

Example 47: Grieg - "Wedding-day at Troldhaugen" (*Lyric Pieces*, Op. 65, no. 6)

Example 48: Rachmaninoff - Prelude in C sharp minor, Op. 3, no. 2

Example 49: Rachmaninoff - Prelude in C sharp minor, Op. 3, no. 2

Example 50: Rachmaninoff - Prelude in C sharp minor, Op. 3, no. 2

Keyboard Stiffness

All pianists, both amateur and professional, have some degree of stiffness in their keyboard approach. Some of this is quite natural and unavoidable due to normal factors such as closeness of hands, articulation of certain notes and chords, and emotional musical response. A very large proportion of players, however, have varying degrees of excessive stiffness in their use of the forearm, especially, even though there is suppleness in the fingers. Finger stiffness, of course, results from neglect of keyboard activity as one progresses through life, even if there are other factors that can result in a similar outcome.

This chapter takes for granted finger suppleness and concentrates on maximum use of the forearm, with its full weight behind every note. A loose and mobile forearm, working in close liaison with the fingers, results in greater freedom and evenness of articulation, better tone control, and (the biggest bonus of all) much less risk of medical problems in this part of the anatomy.

First of all, in sitting at the keyboard, start off by placing the wrist in a comfortable, level to lowly, position in relation to the keys. Aim for a relaxed feeling and test by raising the wrist in an arches, stiffened position to compare the two alternatives. Whilst there will be some unavoidable arching during performance, a lower wrist ensures greater stamina during taxing passages, for example. This will even assist in the octave technique that I will explain a little later here.

Many have witnessed jerky playing, that restricts freedom of coordination as well as even articulation, and some loss of control with musicality, too. In analyzing what actually causes jerkiness, I came to the conclusion that, instead of moving and preparing the forearm into position before the next note or chord, the forearm moved at the same time that the next note or chord was executed.

One of the 'golden' rules of piano playing is that any new note or chord needs to be adequately 'prepared' before it is played, so as to achieve maximum control. With longer note values, the finger would first physically touch and retain contact with a new note, and in doing so, the player could then rotate the wrist several times before actually playing it. This 'stroking' action will then give some better 'feel' for the preparation sensation before moving on to the next note.

Before embarking on a piece, practise a scale very slowly. Whilst the finger is in physical contact with each new note, rhythmically rotate the wrist four times before actually playing it. Hold on the previously played note with one finger in 'preparing' the next unplayed note so as to retain the 'legato' touch. On acquiring a combination of control and comfort the student is now ready to move on to a simple piece.

In *example 51*, by selecting a group of long notes, 'prepare' each half note by rotating the wrist twice before playing it, and do this four times before each whole note, so as to secure the maximum control of the sound that you require.

Again, be sure, though, to hold on to the played note whilst rotating the next unplayed note so as to retain the required 'legato' touch of the piece.

Once the student has acquired this skill it is then time to proceed to the next stage. Before implementing the forearm technique in compositions, it is necessary to start practising a very slow, one-octave scale both separately and together. *Example 52* shows the way to achieve this. Furthermore, one of the benefits of supple forearms is to develop the complete independence of the hands in coordination matters. Here I have indicated the movement of the forearm as it progresses through the scale. A number of things have to be kept in mind in practising the scale, and the very slow tempo will definitely assist in remembering and doing everything at once.

The movement of the forearm should be evenly fluent, never static, which means that it is constantly moving and not subject to 'stops and starts'. As I stated earlier, the full weight must be behind each note, so that the forearm has to move into position behind the note before it is played. To be effective there is only a small movement between each note, otherwise the whole exercise will not function correctly. Keep the wrist low for relaxation purposes, but not unnecessarily so.

Practise the scale hands separately first and, when some confidence is achieved, practise both hands together. You will discover that sometimes both forearms move in the same direction together (easy enough!) but that there are times when they go in opposite directions. If approached in the correct manner, the suppleness of the forearms will encourage complete independence of both hands with coordination.

Of course, each major and minor scale will provide a different formula for the movement of the forearms and this should develop suppleness further. You can stretch the exercise further still by changing normal fingerings of the scales.

I recommend that a portion of the daily practice period/s be allocated to this exercise. The technique can then be implemented in gradual stages with the study of pieces. Do not attempt to play scales or scale passages faster than a tempo of ○=40 at first, but allow patience to prevail in this regard. The technique will eventually absorb naturally into your playing after a while without it being necessary to force progress in any way.

With pieces, the teacher will still have to be vigilant but not over-demanding. Two pieces from *Kinderszenen*, Op. 15 by Robert Schumann could serve as a fairly easy introduction. The first is from "Der Dichter spricht" (**example 53**). Even up to tempo, the player has plenty of time to get both forearms into position in order to 'prepare' succeeding chords. All it takes is a small but significant shift in each case, executed in a gently flowing manner.

Example 54, from "Wichtige Begebenheit", is a more advanced exercise that can be tackled on achieving some level of confidence as a result of practising Example 53.

Do not concern yourself with the left hand octaves approach initially since I intend to discuss this very shortly. Practise the right hand separately, slowly at first, so as to become used to each new shift, but still be careful not to jerk suddenly form one chord to another, To improve the chances of a *cantabile* sound, make sure that the forearm is behind the top note of each chord. Up to tempo, despite the temptation and/or pressure to do otherwise, there is still enough time to shift correctly in advance to each new chord. All this ensures both relaxation and control.

In the last paragraph I promised to describe an octave technique, keeping in mind that such a technique must be able to endure the most demanding of passages. As a matter of interest, one of the biggest challenges in checking the effectiveness of this octave technique is for a performer to 'survive' playing the famous *Erlkönig* by Schubert in a convincing manner, even though it really only taxes one hand! With double octave passages, an immediate candidate for difficulty would be those in Tchaikovsky's *Concerto No. 1 in B flat minor, Op. 23*.

This octave technique is one I embrace wholeheartedly and one that has carried me through successfully in the works I have mentioned. But two factors have to be considered in playing octaves – stamina and speed. With that in mind, I start off by saying that this is a 'sliding' technique, keeping in mind a very familiar keyboard maxim – "the closer you are to the keys, the more control you have over the keys".

Analyzing the technique further, there are several other things to keep in mind with octaves:

- Consciously, keep the wrist as low and relaxed as possible. If tiredness starts to take over, lower the wrist further for relief.

- Break up the whole octave passage into groups of octaves.

- Treat the first note of each group as a 'pivot' octave – (i) lower the arm; (ii) 'prepare' the two notes by half rotating the wrist once whilst retaining physical contact with them; (iii) lean on both octave notes and imagine that an impulse from the arm can then result in a rebounding motion with the remaining octaves in the group: very similar to the rebounding of a ball after the first bounce.

- Have a 'guiding' finger in each hand.

- In the right hand I suggest you guide with the thumb but do not concern yourself too much with the geographical position of the 5th (or 4th) finger since this should largely take care of itself.

- With the left hand, get used to steering with the 5th (or 4th) finger since these fingers tend to get relatively overlooked anyway. Shift the forearm round a little to give more weight support to these fingers also.

- By guiding with the thumb in the right hand and the 5th/4th finger in the left, the guiding process uniformly takes place on the same left side of each hand.

Unfortunately, with octaves, there is definitely some disadvantage having small hands. Fluency is of course affected with the handicap of being unable to use the 4th finger satisfactorily. With younger players, I warn against 'rogue' methods to develop the hands, since this can result in permanent injury. Natural physical development over a period of time can still eliminate such a shortcoming.

When the student is ready to embark on octave playing, I recommend that the first step is to aim at all major and minor keys, separately and together. This will immediately give a range of 36 alternative choices. So far as the 'pivot' octave is concerned, I suggest that the student chooses the keynote each time it occurs. Leaning on this 'pivot' gives the opportunity to activate the arm impulse through another six octaves before the next keynote appears. To give more variety, and provide more 'pivot' opportunities, there is no reason why the octaves should not be broken up into smaller groups.

After a short while of octave scale playing, the student can then think about implementing this technical skill into more practical use. Example 54 focused on the right hand with the intention of using the forearm correctly. As a gentle introduction, *example 55*, which is from the same piece, concentrates on how to execute the left hand in relation to octave playing.

There are several choices open here relating to the placement of pivotal octaves. To avoid an over-rhythmic effect, I suggest that such pivots appear on up-beats. These are ringed in the example, but there is obviously room for pivots on other beats. As confidence grows, then the student will feel like facing octave passages of a more difficult nature.

Two Schubert octave sections, that have some degree of technical dissimilarity, are ones that the intermediate student is bound to encounter at some time. Firstly, *example 56* is from the first movement of the Sonata in A major, D. 664.

The preliminary scale practice should come in very useful here. Low wrists, one 'guiding' finger on the same side of each hand, and the first octave of each group acting as the 'pivot' should really reduce the fairly formidable (to some) nature of the passage. However, those pianists who tend to be a little right-handed will have to ensure that the *fz* beats have less weight in the right hand than in the left. This is achieved by moving the upper part of the body to the left, for better balance, and playing the right hand chords more softly than "what comes naturally".

Example 57 is from the third movement of the D. 664 Sonata; it looks more demanding but its 'sting' can be largely negated with the right approach. First of all, the *fz*s are helpful inasmuch as they are musically more effective if a small pause takes place before each one. This gives more time to prepare the pivots, all of which coincide in both hands with the *fz*s, even though there is some overlap with the time values.

Unless an economical octave technique is employed, still keeping in mind the consistency of low wrists and the maxim "the closer you are to the keys, the more control you have over the keys", I give long odds in maintaining a worthwhile standard in this particularly difficult passage where stamina and speed are so essential.

In this chapter, I have examined two aspects of keyboard stiffness that can have both ineffective and debilitating results on the player. It is highly desirable for the forearm technique to be introduced in the earliest stages of training so as to establish not only good playing habits, but also as some insurance against possible future repetitive strain injury. Similarly, the explained octave technique should ensure maximum relaxation and effectiveness when the student is sufficiently mature and technically advanced.

"All pianists have some degree of stiffness in their keyboard approach"

Keyboard Stiffness – examples

Example 51: Bartók – *Mikrokosmos*, Volume 1

Example 52: Scale of C major M.M. ○ = 40

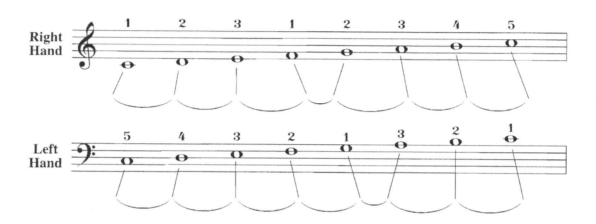

Example 53: Schumann - "Der Dichter spricht" (*Kinderszenen*, Op. 15)

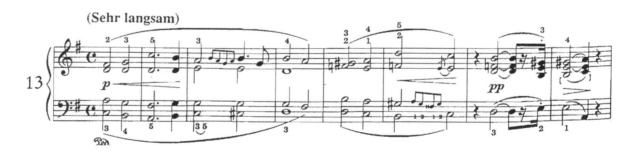

Example 54: Schumann - "Wichtige Begebenheit" (*Kinderszenen*, Op. 15)

Example 55: Schumann - "Wichtige Begebenheit" (*Kinderszenen*, Op. 15)

Example 56: Schubert - Sonata in A major, D. 664 (first movement)

Example 57: Schubert - Sonata in A minor, D. 784 (third movement)

33

Cross-Rhythms

One of the most frequently encountered 'hurdles' in piano playing is the articulation of cross-rhythms. By this I refer to opposing rhythms, mostly between the right and left hands, that are not mathematically symmetrical. In many cases, students find this a 'grey' area and one that is often too intimidating to face. Yet, approached in a calm, methodical way, cross-rhythms can be easily coped with, even leading to a sense of satisfaction in executing them successfully.

The most basic cross-rhythm is three notes against two notes, a situation that occurs with great regularity in keyboard works. Less frequent is 4/3, and from then one can be asked to come to grips on occasion with even more complex relationships than that.

All the examples in this chapter come from the Chopin *Nocturnes* where the composer makes numerous and highly varied cross-rhythm demands on his interpreters. In the Nocturne in E minor, Op. 72, no. 1, for instance, there is a sequence of 4/3, 8/3 and 10/3 cross-rhythms in quick succession.

So, what is the strategy in dealing with this? The first task is to clarify the mathematical note positioning between the rhythms. In the case of 3/2, the second of the duplet notes comes between the second and third notes of the triplet figure. Thus *example 60*, bar 11 of the Nocturne in B flat minor, Op. 9, no. 1.

With 4/3, the second note of the triplet figure comes between the second and third notes of the quadruplet figure, with the fourth note of the quadruplets appearing after the last of the triplet notes. We see this in *example 61*, bar 34 of the Nocturne in B major, Op. 9, no. 3.

With 5/4, after the two hands play the first notes together, the second note in the group with the greater number of notes comes next. The remaining notes are then exchanged between the hands in a split but consistent manner until the last of the quintuplets is played following the last of the quadruplets. A similar approach, with sextuplets and septuplets, follows with 7/6. This is illustrated in *example 62*, from bar 75 of the Nocturne in D flat major, Op. 27, no. 2.

At this point I should mention that where both groups can be exactly subdivided, then that should take place before note-splitting is finally completed. In bar 3 of the B flat minor Nocturne, we have a group of 22 notes in the right hand and 12 notes in the left hand; the exact subdivisions are, of course, 2 groups of 11 and 6 notes respectively. This is demonstrated in *example 63*.

In another Nocturne (in B major, Op. 62, no. 1), Chopin unhelpfully places 41 notes against 4! This obviously cannot be subdivided, yet both hands still need to coordinate in a satisfactory, musical manner. My suggested solution is not completely accurate mathematically, but I believe it works well musically, taking into account the melodic flow of the passage, and it is shown in *example 64*, commencing at bar 26.

As with most things in life, there is nearly always an exception to every rule. For instance, refer to an excerpt (shown in *examples 65/66*) from the well-known F sharp major Nocturne, Op. 15, no. 2, which was a favorite of the renowned Chopin interpreter, Artur Rubinstein.

Mathematically, this is an exact division of 10/1 since the whole group places 40 notes against 4 and is, strictly speaking, not a cross-rhythm, but to reconcile this musically is not so straightforward. The first block of 18 notes of the 40-note group are shaped as triplets and the remaining block of 22 act as a resolution factor. To capture the decorative yet improvised character of the music, small adjustments to where the left hand fits in need to be made, otherwise the result will be too mechanical and jerky. Here, in effect, one has created a 'cross-rhythm' for artistic purposes.

Example 65 shows the mathematical division and *example 66* demonstrates my musical solution. Let me quickly add, however, that the latter is a subjective solution and that others may well wish to adopt a solution of their own, with an appropriate alternative version. Such is the joy of interpretation!

At this point, after a lifetime of teaching and playing, I wish to offer an opinion about the musical execution of cross-rhythms. I believe that music, being an expressive art, cannot be approached in a purely mechanical, over-rhythmic manner. The use of rubato is always present and governs every moment of musical interpretation to a lesser or greater degree. I further believe that the only way to cope successfully with a cross-rhythm is to have one group played in a fairly even manner, with the other group being subservient in an accommodating yet relatively uneven way. If I can illustrate the latter with an analogy, imagine an intoxicated person (the uneven group) walking and lurching to some extent whilst constantly grabbing on a hand-rail (the even group) for assistance.

Having said that, the question is posed as to which hand is the even one and which is the uneven. At the risk of sounding evasive, I have discovered that there is no hard and fast rule. A decision has to be made as to what best serves the musical flow. Sometimes the left hand accompanying line is the 'straighter' of the two (again, see *example 60*). Yet, in bar 3 of the same Nocturne, the right hand melodic line seems to work in a more flowing and unstilted manner if played 'straighter' (see *example 63*).

Cross-rhythms form an area of technique that often receives little focus and attention; as a result, some student pianists tend to bluster or fake their way through them if ignorance or fear has set in. But, if a player is to be accomplished at a high level then an informed method of approach has to take place if the musical demands are to be met satisfactorily.

"Cross-rhythms can be easily coped with"

Cross-Rhythms – examples

Example 60: Chopin - *Nocturne* in B flat minor, op. 9 no. 1

Example 61: Chopin - *Nocturne* in B major, op. 9 no. 3

Example 62: Chopin - *Nocturne* in D flat major, op. 27 no. 2

Example 63: Chopin - *Nocturne* in B flat minor, op. 9 no. 1

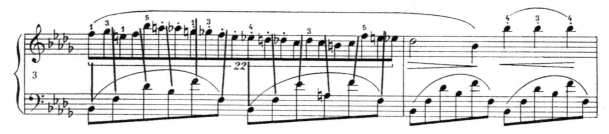

Example 64: Chopin - *Nocturne* in B major, op. 62 no. 1

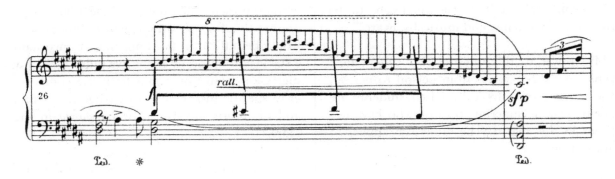

Example 65: Chopin - *Nocturne* in F sharp major, op. 15 no. 2

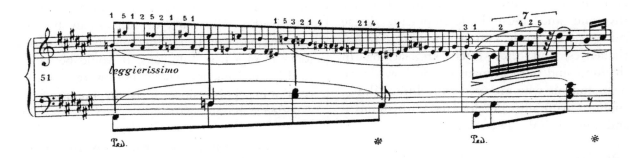

Example 66: Chopin - *Nocturne* in F sharp major, op. 15 no. 2

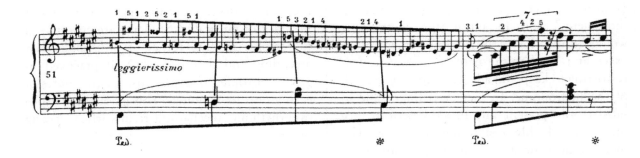

Developing technique into musicality

"Is a physically gifted student likely to be rhythmically reliable and musically aware?"

My answer to this question is, "Often, no." Sense of rhythm varies from person to person, and some more physically gifted students are not necessarily superior to those who have less talent in this regard. The same also applies to musical awareness.

While some students are naturally gifted, they often develop these "gifts" through extensive technical practice and training. Unfortunately, there are many instances where this training is done in a mechanical fashion that hampers rhythmic and musical development. These students can easily conquer tough technical challenges, but they often are lacking in rhythmic and musical maturity. So how do we help students who are used to technical things coming "naturally" develop more rhythmic – and thus musical – awareness?

Rhythm, of course, is the most important element of music-making, and it also governs every aspect of life. Because of this, every living creature is affected by it and exhibits awareness of it to a certain degree. *The Concise Oxford Dictionary* refers to rhythm as "metrical movement," and in music the metronome would be the closest thing to movement of an exact and mechanical nature. However, it is restricting to keep and adhere to the regular tick of the metronome. In fact, it is impossible to satisfactorily present any musical performance under this highly restraining influence. The metronome cannot be our only approach to shoring up rhythmic deficiencies.

Rubato in daily life

So how does one get around it? In music the term that refers to establishing a coherent flow of phrasing is called *rubato*. This Italian word, meaning "robbed," refers to adjustments of speed – constant accelerations and decelerations of pace – that enhance musical expression within an established meter. These adjustments are mostly of a very minor nature, otherwise it would be difficult if not impossible to maintain a stable and musically expressive pulse. The only digression from this would be if the composer gives specific instructions to change the tempo and/or inserts *accelerando* or *ritardando* in the score.

If one thinks about it, *rubato* dominates everyone in daily life in whatever activity one is engaged. Without *rubato*, one just could not exist. Think of the uneven way a person breathes, talks, walks, or runs, no matter how slightly or extremely such actions are achieved. To breathe, talk, walk, or run exactly like a metronome would certainly result in strange looks from aghast onlookers. It would be hard to discover someone who is not aware of life's continuing pulse since it is an ever-present experience in one's existence.

Mechanical scale practice can delay rhythmic and musical growth

Rhythm is certainly a feature of the early years for piano students. Unfortunately though, the conventional way that scales are practiced over the years to develop the fingers can often result in a lack of musicality. Students are encouraged to emphasize the tonic of a scale when ascending and descending. Or if practiced in groups of triplets or sixteenths, the first notes of each group are accented. This gradually leads to over-rhythmic, mechanical results when playing pieces.

One general suggestion that I make to students about the pulse is to feel as few strong beats to the bar as possible, even in a very slow piece. By adopting this policy the movement of the music flows more naturally instead of in a stilted fashion.

Listening to international piano competitions can be quite revealing. There are often two outcomes in how gifted and advanced young performers approach their work. One is how metronomic the playing can be. Alternatively, the fingers can often be heard skidding over the keys in an indistinct manner with little regard to a consistent musical pulse. This may be an unconscious sort of rebellion against the years of practicing scales in an isolated environment. Tone control is often the last aspect to receive attention in a pianist's training (for reasons that are incomprehensible to me), and thus is also something that is frequently lacking. For example, it is a regular experience for *p* to sound *pp* or even *ppp* from players who otherwise have very advanced technical skill.

In listening to the recent Sydney International Piano Competition of Australia I found that the over-rhythmic habit of giving precedence to main beats was particularly exposed in the playing of works by composers such as Mozart and Haydn, whose music should be more transparent.

Practice solutions

I believe that from very early on, a student should be encouraged to practice scales in a slow manner by accenting offbeat notes. As the student progresses, they should then get rid of these accents (these practice steps develop control) and shape the scale into a more melodic line. For instance, in groups of three try emphasizing the second note of the triplet figure, and then the third note. To make it more interesting in a scale that is ascending and descending, one can alternate between the two. The same approach can be extended to mordents and slow trills where temporary accents can be placed on notes other than the ones on downbeats. Of course, by all means practice the traditional methods of accenting the tonic and/or the first notes of triplets and sixteenths, but broaden the approach. By doing this a sense of phrasing can be instilled early on instead of many years later, if ever.

Composers are not always accommodating in starting the first note of phrases on a main beat (thank goodness!). Since technical work should be preparation for playing pieces and not treated as an end in itself, in my view it is imperative to keep all this in mind. Frequently a melodic phrase overlaps a bar line but often this does not deter a young performer from accenting the downbeat in the middle of it. What happens? The phrase becomes bumpy and uneven. The answer is to gently but firmly emphasize the first note of the phrase that will coincide with an upbeat, and then flow into the next bar in a smooth and musical manner.

To further assist getting the feel of phrasing in playing beyond main beats, listen to an accomplished singer or string quartet to hear how they express their music in a *cantabile* manner. It can be helpful if you listen to music of a slow-moving pace at first and then move on to faster tempi. As you practice faster in your own playing, or if you are fearful of losing the natural pulse, place a very small pause at the bar line to re-establish the basic meter. Eventually you will be in less need of this and should ultimately be able to discard it.

Small pauses for *sforzandi*

It is amazing what very small pauses in phrasing can achieve. One frequently hears a *sforzando* given a heavy accent, for example. This may be justified in a certain context, but the degree of emphasis is often unnecessary. In this dilemma I have encouraged students to overcome such a heavy-handed approach by adopting three different ways of dealing with a *sforzando*:

1. Place a very small pause before it and play the note with no accent at all. This action (called an agogic accent) will result in an accent being implied; *or*

2. Place a very small pause and give a gentle accent; *or*

3. In more extreme circumstances, give a firmer accent in addition to the pause (even then the tone should not be unduly forced).

. . . and syncopations

Young players, especially in ensemble situations, often have difficulties with syncopations, and they end up playing with distorted rhythms. The solution is very similar to that of a *sforzando*. In a jazz piece one frequently encounters an off-beat note that is tied to a main beat note. Instead of playing the off-beat with a large accent and thereby throwing the pulse into disarray, only a small adjustment needs to be made. By all means accent the off-beat note but insert a very small pause just before the main beat to re-establish the pulse. This will stabilize the performance, respect the composer's intentions, and everyone will end up being happy!

Another syncopation problem that one encounters in 6/8 is when there are three quarter notes in one hand and six eighth notes in the other. Frequently the performer goes from two groups of three to three groups of two, thereby ending up in 3/4. The rhythmic distortion is glaring and quite unnecessary. Again, there is a simple solution. By inserting a tiny pause after the second of the quarter notes (halfway across the measure), the 6/8 meter is clearly communicated and the syncopation is made effective. The same approach can be used in other situations where a syncopation "threatens" to disrupt the rhythmic flow.

Ensemble playing must also "breathe"

If a student wishes to be an accomplished musical player, dealing with the complex situation of rhythm has to be addressed. In an ensemble scenario, including performing as soloist with an orchestra, a performer has to be utterly clear in regards to both rhythm and musicality.

I remember many years ago I had an unpleasant run-in with a conductor when I was engaged to make a radio recording of Rachmaninoff's *Rhapsody on a Theme of Paganini, Op. 43*. During a rehearsal, in starting the first of the more rhapsodic variations, the conductor turned and accused me of "playing out of time" in front of the entire orchestra. I felt sufficiently confident to stand my ground, but the accusation was not withdrawn. Eventually, I had no alternative but to walk back to the dressing room. During the rehearsal break, the concertmaster of the orchestra came to see me and assured me that they could follow me perfectly, and that the conductor was not held in high regard by the players. I was also told the producer approached the conductor and informed him that unless the recording was completed he would forfeit his fee. A meeting was arranged between us forthwith. Following a piano rehearsal, the recording was completed without a further hitch. However, that experience is not something I would want to repeat in a hurry!

In summing up my response to the question of this article, I wish to urge students to keep the application of rhythm in perspective. Yes, it is certainly the most important aspect of music-making, but the use of it has to be applied in a sensible manner – otherwise the music suffers. Students often become victims of rhythmic tyranny because the development of technique becomes an obsession through all the years of hard work. Technique has to be the servant of musical expression, not the master, and technical practice should be kept in proper perspective by treating it only as preparation for the playing of pieces.

I hope I have shown that good rhythmic playing is not necessarily straightforward, and that natural physical talent is not necessarily a guarantee of good music-making. However, in the situation where a gifted student is lacking in musical subtlety because of a misguided use of rhythm, there is no reason why the problem cannot be successfully addressed under the tutelage of an effective teacher.

"Technique has to be the servant of musical expression, not the master"

Lightning Source UK Ltd.
Milton Keynes UK
UKHW051132291022
411223UK00010B/51